T0066786

Sacred Bonds

Sacred Bonds

An Essay in Relationships

Kalyani R Menon

PARTRIDGE

Copyright © 2016 by Kalyani R Menon.

ISBN:	Softcover	978-1-4828-7359-7
	eBook	978-1-4828-7358-0

All rights reserved. No part of this book may be used or reproduced by any means, graphic, electronic, or mechanical, including photocopying, recording, taping or by any information storage retrieval system without the written permission of the author except in the case of brief quotations embodied in critical articles and reviews.

Because of the dynamic nature of the Internet, any web addresses or links contained in this book may have changed since publication and may no longer be valid. The views expressed in this work are solely those of the author and do not necessarily reflect the views of the publisher, and the publisher hereby disclaims any responsibility for them.

Print information available on the last page.

To order additional copies of this book, contact
Partridge India
000 800 10062 62
orders.india@partridgepublishing.com

www.partridgepublishing.com/india

CONTENTS

Section I
Beyond Pali Hill

Section II
Labour of Love

Section III
Hopes for Another Day

To

My son, Ashwat

ACKNOWLEDGEMENTS

This book would not have been possible but for the unstinted cooperation and support of my family. My husband and son gave me all the time and freedom to take off from duties at home to concentrate on producing this work. My mother heard at random some of the writings that I read aloud and encouraged me to move further.

I must thank my father for being with me all the way and goading me into this work. He has been my mentor and my guide and has taken pains to proofread and go through every chapter.

I must add here that publishing became a serious thought when I joined a newly formed Writers Group. It was a closed group which met every week to discuss our own writings and to support each other in translating our thoughts into words. Had it not been for their encouragement and appreciation, I would not have had the courage to think in terms of publishing this book. My association with the members of this group has indeed been highly instructive. I would like to particularly thank Mr Bharat Sethuraman who has been the driving force behind the Writers Group and who has prevailed upon me to keep writing.

My association with people has given me fruitful experiences to know what to do and what not to do. They all have a part in the making of this book. The Almighty has given me a second chance to live and savour life's sweetness. I am eternally grateful to Him and value it for having made me flower and revel in its unprepared celebrations.

INTRODUCTION

An introduction to this book is necessary because without it the reader will not be able to appreciate the reasons for my urge to publish it. This is not a collection of assorted and unrelated jottings. It has grown out of my own growth from innocent childhood through the pains of entering adulthood in a complex and confusing urban setting.

Through my book I would like to reach out to people and through their love and acceptance I would be motivated to write further.

My childhood began in the posh surroundings of Pali Hill where my father lived in a company flat. I saw many figures and fantasisedmany events in th e cosy nest that was the Pali Hill home. I soon realised that life had more dimensions than that nest could show me and that I had to fly out of it to breathe fresh air. The first part of my book is therefore titled Beyond Pali Hill. It contains images that were very close to my heart, images that helped me to see slices of another world.

As I grew through the pains of adulthood, I had to make many sacrifices but at the end of it I found that they gave me the strength to face life and determination to live for a purpose and to try to find meaning in my own life. That meaning came largely through my own family and my loved ones. They gave support and succour and through my many moods I was able to see and understand what love really meant. My own son, husband, father and mother taught me that lesson in love and helped me to mould my personality. The second part is therefore devoted to my eternal love for the divinity within them that drove me to them. A casual reader may construe this as an obsessive love of the family; it is only my gratitude to The Almighty for having given me the family that would make me what I am today.

A product of all this has been my own thoughts about varied subjects that have influenced my life and actions. Be it vegetarianism, care of women and the disadvantaged, I have been driven by strong feelings. These are not uncommon although they may be controversial. I would offer them as the outpourings of an anguished soul. The third part therefore contains these outpourings.

I must add that this book has tried to its utmost not to hurt anyone's feelings; if it spreads goodwill and affection I shall consider myself blessed.

Kalyani

CHAPTER 1

AN IMAGE EMBALMED

"Yourself or outside, you never have to change what you see, only the way you see it."

Thaddeus Golas

The school exams were over. I lived a bored life in a cocoon of comfort, doing private nothings and indulging in strange delusions. I was thirteen, an awkward age and what I thought or did mattered little to any one else.

In my unpredictable life, I had a compulsive urge to surrender to irrational thoughts and feelings. Weird imaginings overflowed from occasional streaks of insanity like molten lava from a volcanic eruption. I remained for the most part wrapped in myself, insensitive to the world outside.

Yet my insensitive eyes could not be totally blind to some glimpses of shooting pain, loneliness and emotional outbursts of others. I guess these have left a scar on me.

My balcony at Pali Hill overlooked the sea on one side and the narrow dug up Pali Mala Road on the other. "Tofa Tofa, laaya laaya" rang a screeching sound one afternoon like a painful ad jingle, intruding into my treasured moments of peace and privacy. I came out only to sculpt a little angel swaying in the middle of the street. This barely nine year old babe played on a miniature drum striking it with all his spite. He continued this unending, unrehearsed melody, painful to my ears and wasted on a sleepy side road.

"Main Bhairu hoon, Bheeru nai" yelled the angel a song later, adding that Manu his friend had tagged to him the label of a coward.

My impatient hands chose to quickly close the windows and shut out the noise. In that mood I would not have acted differently had it been Lata Mangeshkar with a tanpura although the so called elite would have come out in full force from their house to swing to her bhajans.

Just then curiosity took the better of me and as I peeped out there was Heeera, our Bhairu's mate and mentor, lifting her left foot, on an aluminium plate, moving the right foot too and moving in circles as one possessed. Her intricate steps and near pefect rhythm more than matched Bhairu's music. As she swung her little plait, Heeera danced with a zeal that I as a student of dance did never have. Not a trace of self pity on her face, no melancholy in the monotony of Bhairu's lines.

Looking down I asked, "Bhairu, where are your parents." And added rather foolishly, "Do they let you do this?"

Grabbing his little drum and clutching on to Heera's choli with the other, Bhairu was moving swiftly down the street.

I flashed a crisp note for them and repeated the question expecting the sniff of money to do the rest.

Looking up to the heavens Bhairu said, "My parents are out there twinkling like stars. When we grow old we too will go and shine. I have heard it is a heaven with plentiful Dahivadas, Panipuris which Shyamlal the kanjoos denies us. We will then be forbidden from entertaining these crowds. Crowds! Hee! Hee! Our market is any way down. It is all break dance now. Heera wants me to study but we don't earn enough"

The icy cold Heeera wore a frozen visage. The look of royal sympathy on my amused face angered her. I offered one more crisp note. "You have come to stop us haven't you? A public nuisance you consider us? We are here to be recognized for our singing, some direct lifts from films and some original compositions of Heera, Bhairu and Manu." She added, "We do live in our special dreams as you do …someday a music director will come to us and with a little training we will be on the stage to receive a standing ovation. Heera's voice will be not a croaking frog's voice but a nightingale's." With a sudden contemptuous look she added, "please give your worthless notes to beggars. We aren't beggars, we are artistes. Chalo Bhairu". What an outpouring of silent anguish!. Nothing could have so forcefully shown me the worthlessness of my own existence.

Looking back through the long tunnel of time, Bhairu's Dum Dum and Heeera's De De Pyar De have come back to me as sweet, sad melodies in moments of utter melancholy.

I have not met them again. Several years later, I did run into a familiar figure one grey evening. It was at a wedding reception in Bandra. As I moved to wash my hands after dinner I heard a voice call out "O Manu, jaldi aa". Yes, it was Manu, now grown up, shy and strangely quiet, cleaning vessels at a furious pace. I walked up to him and asked

"Where are Heera and Bhairu"?

Heera was married off to an old man. And Bhairu? Opening his arms wide open and looking up he said, "Wo Chala Gaya, Chala Gaya".

Perhaps, Bhairu was up there, with Dahivadas and Panipuris which Shyamlal never gave him, twinklig like a star and forbidden to sing.!

Bhairu and Heeera, your angelic persona has filled a vacuum in my heart. Thank you Bhairu, thank you Heeera for lifting a torch beyond the streets of Pali Hill.

CHAPTER 2

FORTUNE'S HALF SMILE

"Thousands of candles can be lighted from a single candle and the life of the candle will not be shortened. Happiness never decreases by being shared."

Budha

Gazing at the sky, Daisy could see the clouds threatening to set in as she hastened to rush to her spacious villa to close the doors and windows before the massive downpour could begin. Cheerful as she was always, she paced up and down her garden collecting colourful flowers, sweet fragrance that with the sandalwood incence would be her offering to her Lord Jesus. She trusted her Merciful Lord who, she was convinced, would help her from falling apart. Her prime responsibilitynow was to uplift her ailing husband's spirits and to boost his morale. To Patrick, Daisy was the sole source of strength, his moral support, with whom he had tied the nuptial knot when Daisy was 19 and Patrick was 21. They had three beautiful children. Daisy stood by him stoically to shoulder difficult times with a radiant smile. For her lovable children she had learnt to make beautiful cake, toys and odd decoration materials. Now that has come in handy both to earn an income and to showcas e her talents.

Under Daisy's alluring shadow, her three doted children excelled in both academics and extracurricular activities. On learning that her only daughter Serena was taking part in a school dance competition, Daisy herself tailored for her a gorgeous pink dress with awesome frills and a satin bow with matching pink velvet dancing shoes. It was a day to remember when Serena was nominated and got the winner of the year trophy for her dancing skills -undoubtedly the best performance of the evening. Daisy was overjoyed and the family celebrated Serena's success with a special dinner exclusively prepared by Daisy herself.

Patrick congratulated Daisy with a look of absolute contentment and peace saying "You are our angel, our guardian angel, taking such good patient care of us... Because of you, Daisy, our children are learning to be independent -at an age when they can easily falter, be misguided. Behind their success you are the guiding light. Hats off to you, a Big Thank You." Hearing these words of undiluted admiration, Daisy's eyes brimmed with tears of unexplainable joy and gratitude. She told herself this is her true reward.

Patrick and Daisy lived with their three children in Patrick's ancestral home down Pali Hill. It was considered a posh area, to which had migrated film stars, business executives and wealthy traders. The east Indian cottages that populated the place had given place to high rise apartments. Patrick's two storied house, with the garden that was his father's pride, stood in marked isolation. Not that it was not being eyed by real estate sharks-Patrick had received several offers, and even threats ; recent calls that were abusive and alarming made him cut off his telephone connection altogether! There was even a big debate in the family on whether they needed a telephone. Daisy won the day with the solid support of the children and the connection was restored.

The rent frrom the tenant above was a meagre Rs 600 and wasn't enough even to cover the childrens pocket money. When Patrick was strong and healthy he could work out a handsome salary from his job in railways. He was well thought of and had every hope of success in his career. "will never, never give in to the sharks," he thought.

Patrick often watched the tide rise on the Bandra coast. He had also watched it ebb. The tide had risen in his life too. "The inevitable ebb too has begun "he thought. For, things had changed:he was incapacitated and no longer a picture of perfect health. Forced to retire from railways, he had to now plan a life based on a modest pension. He would help Daisy in all creative earning activities that she was planning to start.

Back home from the bazaar, while busy with the vegetables and arranging the day's purchases, Daisy heard a disturbed Serena call out, "Mamma, Reena (my friend) who lives right opposite is extremely grieved: her parents have met with a serious accident and are reportedly recovering slowly in a hospital in Bangalore." Daisy had known of Reena and had even seen her once in her school in the company of other children. She knew that Reena was barely 13 yrs and came from an affluent family. She was now uncertain of her parents' future, even of their coming out of the gruesome road accident they had on way down from Ooty. She was forced to manage her daily life all alone -taking care of her home, of herself and her studies with extreme anxiety. She spent the day all alone, lost in fear of an uncertain future.

Peeping out of her window, Daisy watched Reena looking down from her balcony, reading aloud from her book, teary eyed, looking lost. Daisy could well feel her pain and loneliness as her own.

Daisy immediately said to Serena, "Serena, Go, talk to Reena, persuade her to take time off and to come over".

One look at Serena and Reena bent down to her knees and cried profusely giving vent to her pentup sorrow and disdain. She did not move.

Patrick called out to Daisy, "Daisy, here is a helpless girl who urgently needs a mother's care and love : I know you can give it better than anyone!." The following day, Daisy mustered courage to search for Reena's flat. She saw the nameplate "The Mehtas" and knew that was where Reena lived although there was another Mehta in the same building. Daisy knocked on Reena's door. She thought of Reena's desperation, of her waking hours and even her dreams when she would be missing her parents and her parents in turn would be longing to comfort her. With bated breath, Daisy waited patiently outside for Reena to open the door to her room and indeed to her little world. Reena cautiously peeped through the door, recognized Daisy and welcomed her with a faint half-smile. Seating herself on a rickety chair, Daisy looked closely into Reena's pale face and her simple appearance, in a traditional dress with long flowing tresses tied in a firm plait. Reena touched Daisy's hand nervously and cried bitterly saying her parents had met with a road accident, were seriously injured too, and would take a awhile to recover from mental and physical scars.

Daisy couldn't hide her tears too. She drew Reena close to her in a tight embrace and said, "Reena my girl, don't be heartbroken; give me your pain so that you are relieved from it. Please don't worry. We are all with you, in your pain and sorrow. We share your grief." Daisy smothered Reena with sweet kisses on her forhead and hugging her again, slowly walked back to her quiet villa with an emptiness she had never experienced before.

Daisy wanted to spread her wings to protect this teenaged girl in distress. Reena was surely a brave girl, living alone without the help from neighbours, relatives or friends. Soon Daisy was swept with a strong sense of attachment to Reena.

Daisy was now approaching the day when she could prove her love to Reena.

On Sunday 16th September, Daisy and her children left for the church dressed in all their finery. On their way back, Serena said, "Mama, today is 16th, Reena's birthday!th. Serena knew her mother would come up with something to surprise her friend. Daisy often prided herself on giving such surprises and would not let go of an opportunity. She quickly opened her huge chest in which she had stored several artifacts and spotted in a corner, a red jewellery box made of cardboard, one she had made around last Christmas. It was a nicely decorated jewellery box with compartments that could store Reena's bangles and earrings. Daisy guessed this would be an handsome gift.

Daisy scurried to clean her house with a steady broom in one hand and a bottle of phenyle in the other. On any other day, this would have been a daily, dreary chore. Not today : it was a labour of love.

Daisy could well imagine how much Reena would be missing her parents -who would have thought of celebrating her birthday with pomp and splendour.

In a reclining chair in her balcony, Reena looked on as several young men and women emerged in the street festive colours to take a huge Ganesha idol for immersion. Bandra. It seemed an endless procession of old devotees and young merrymakers in and following huge trucks carrying the Ganesha idol. She had seen this year after year…and would see it again next year! But would her parents be with her? Reena sank into despair on her own plight – wholly out of tune, with the celebration outside. She needed her parents more than ever before, who may now be writhing in agony.

Meanwhile, Daisy decorated the inner living room with paper scrolls and designer flatoons. Her sons, Jason and Jackson readied the music system and promptly blew huge balloons which were suspended from the sides of the newly painted walls. The table was dressed with a lacy table cloth, with a healthy spread of marshmellows, jam tarts, and puffs with many snacks, sweets and juices, all personally prepared or procured by Daisy. She wanted to remember everything to the minutest detail. She wanted the cake to be the best she had ever made. She baked a sumptous goodlooking fluffy chocolate cake, writing with a pink icing on it "Happy birthday Reena" This was the message the family wanted to put across to the girl who had walked into their lives and hearts.

It was 5 pm and the procession was getting denser by the minute. Daisy cut across to get to the other side of the road and into Reena's apartment. At the third knock, Reena opened her door cautiously to find Daisy present with a bouquet of fragrant flowers. Reena drew her arms around Daisy. Daisy invited Reena hoping she would at last come and spend sometime with them. With a sweet shy smile Reena nodded her head and said "Yes".

Casually dressed Reena arrived hesitantly to be welcomed with a loud melodious "Happy Birthday to you "from Daisy and family who held her dainty hands and wished her earnestly one after the other. As she entered their home, to her total amazement, she found her classmates all springing to their feet to wish her. They had specially been invited and sat next to the table where the cake was kept. Reena was baffled as her hazel eyes gazed at her classmates, her friends, Daisy and Serena, Patrick, Jason and Jackson. Daisy, who had seen Reena for the first time only a month ago, had done all this to make her feel loved, cared and wanted.

Music played in the background with an exuberance Reena yet had to feel, absorb and cherish- as she stepped into the dance floor, untying her hair and dancing uninhibitedly. So did her friends and the family in a memorable unabashed dance of joy. Later, As she blew the candles, she was encircled by happiness all around her. Reena spoke to herself "These are the messengers from God living moment after moment to see me alive and breathing, safe and sound. What have I done to receive such affection and acceptance. Surely this is a blessing from the Almighty."

As the candles were being lit for the second time, this time to thank the Lord, Reena prayed bowing with gratitude to Daisy and her family who accepted her as their own, who expected nothing and gave so much, attaching no name to their relationship. There was an unwritten, unexplained bond between them. She thought there were people in this magnificent world who could make a difference, add a new meaning to our lives. It's not their wealth, standing or status that mattered but their compassion, consideration, and insight into the life of a lonely girl who grieved for what she did'nt get and received what she did'nt expect.

CHAPTER 3

THE CHOSEN ONE

*"Love is the only wayto grasp another human
being in the innermost core of his personality"*

Viktor Frankl

Mr. and Mrs. Nair were an inseparable couple living primarily for each other; in the absence of one, the other's life would be meaningless. Their love for one another was inexpressible; together they laughed off their worries and preserved a sacred bond that death could perhaps not sever...They felt intensely that all children were their own. A childless couple, they felt deeply and even moaned to friends that they had missed hearing the first cry of a baby, the elation of carrying the extension of their own flesh and blood in their eager arms, missed the warmth and excitement, if they had a little cradle kept rocking, with the baby gurgling, with sparkling eyes; missed the sheer amusement and fortune to be parents of a prized possession.

It was springtime, neither cold nor warm; new and fresh marigolds, jasmines blossomed, deserting the wilted ones. A pleasant change of season was like a refreshingly picturesque masterpiece of a painter on a grand canvas. It was an unusually bright sunny day, Mr. Nair, adjusting his tight rimmed glasses, was lost in thought about the political scenario in the country; reading the newspaper with avid interest, relaxing in his reclining chair, he wondered aloud, how if the country was in such appalling state, we could trust and elect any person into power- who would be respected and saluted along with the national flag.

Mrs. Nair was dicing vegetables to make a special mixed vegetable curry. Just then the doorbell rang and she opened it to be greeted by an irresistible, handsome young man in his early twenties, wearing a shiny jacket with matching jeans, presenting a face so endearing, with an enigmatic dashing personality. On enquiring, he said he was their close friend's son Rohan. Mrs Nair's intuitive mind told her that they would soon be swept off their feet that she would love to attach him to her apron strings as most mothers do. She would be so indulgent as to want her son or daughter be dependent on the mother till they chose to fly away like a cuckoo from its nest.

The time sped fast and Rohan enthralled them with his bubbly enthusiasm, and liveliness, entertaining them with interesting stories, reviving memories of his school days, of his humorous encounters with people and even mimicking celebrities. They looked mesmerized and lost in total admiration and love.

It was dinnertime and Rohan dashed to the kitchen even before Mrs. Nair did, carrying the dishes, laying the table and serving them food as they ate with a strange feeling of joy and delirium. Food tasted exceptionally good today, they judged. They have never had such an experience. Here was a boy, not a familiar face four days ago, but one of their own now. A boy after their own heart, one they would have liked to have if by God's grace they had one. A God send indeed! Rohan was considerate and concerned to the extreme about the little things that lighted up their lives that could erase completely, though momentarily, the melancholic emptiness of their lives.

A click of a button and Mr. and Mrs. Nair were photographed in a romantic pose, and with a selfie aid, three of them were captured in a photo with Rohan fondly drawing them closer to him, a picture of completeness and intense pleasure, an experience, only an offspring can give to fill a vast vacuum. He was not born to them but at this moment was more than a son to them. He too felt they were his own parents in the secrecy of this private villa, which could be a permanent abode for him in time to come. Overcome by strong maternal instincts, Mrs. Nair stroked Rohan's hair while he blissfully tossed and turned in her lap like a child who was delivered from her womb. Rohan could feel her immobilized pain; he had come to wipe her tears. Rohan whispered 'Amma' into her receptive ears. She felt as though all the bells in the shrine were ringing simultaneously. This was one extraordinary experience they wouldn't exchange for anything in the world, so real, so baffling, so pure and precious, unspoken and unspeakable.

As the Nairs tucked the sheets for Rohan's bed, later in the evening, they arranged the pillows, kept a jug of water by the bedside, were about to switch off the table lamp, when to their utter surprise they were feathered by soft goodnight kisses on both sides of their cheeks in turns before Rohan went under the crisp cotton white sheets to sleep.

Even in his sleep there was an aura of a glowing light, a smiling face, blessed and unspoilt and untouched. It was so inviting, they had a sudden urge to hold him close to them, and pat him slowly till he slept. Could they do so and how long could they? They had promised themselves that they would not question but be thankful for these pleasurable moments of experienced parenthood – once in a lifetime- without asking for it or pleading for one...........

Rohan's short stay was about to end. By now he was enveloped in sacred love, too deep to fathom. They knew that he would be gone soon. For hours, no words passed between him and his new found parents and yet they struck a strange, silent wave that moved back and forth between their minds.

Rohan dreaded going back to Bangalore, to two broken homes where his estranged parents lived. In his early years he was the sole witness to sparks that flew and frequent wordy duels. It never got violent except perhaps once: it was a faint memory but one he could not erase from his mind. The bickering would be followed by long periods of silence, which was even more insufferable. In the midst of their quarrels, Rohan felt rejected.

Strangely, both his father and mother spoke to him highly of the Nairs. They thought it would be nice if Rohan could visit them. For Rohan it was a blessing in disguise; it could unburden him of a strange mixture of feelings of neglect, free him from his parents whom he could not hug when he needed them most; from whom he had not a gentle whisper of affection, a caressing touch. The separation between his parents was like a sharp knife moving right through his heart; not that they didn't love him, but that they were too preoccupied with their own fancied lifestyle, in a social circle that Rohan found too hybrid, unreal. There was a marked difference between them and the Nairs who loved and could show love through simple acts and gestures. His parents, the Nambiars, could only think of their own careers and individual interests which had no meeting point: he remembered pleading once for reunion to save himself, their only son, from embarrassment; and remembered the look on their faces which explained their innermost feeling of mutual hatred.

Here at Nairs, Rohan was having a time of his life: he stacked their suitcases on the loft; pressed Mrs. Nair's tired feet, enjoying a game of cricket; for every six or four they would scream in ecstasy, holding each other in a tight embrace. When Mrs. Nair prepared his favorite moru curry, it would appear that, as if from nowhere, the tantalizing aroma lingered much after he had had his fill of that steamed curry. Squatting on a colorful mat on the floor, Rohan would break into an English song in praise of The Nairs, pouring his heart out. He would tell them how much they meant to him; when he was parched up, they gave him a free flowing river to quench his thirst. He thought he had been introduced to a new world that was moulding his personality anew and giving his life a new definition, a security, he had craved for.

The Nairs were at an emotional crossroads in their lives. They couldn't help wondering whether Rohan's memorable stay would be short lived; will they be able to see him again? Rohan was now the center of their universe, their walking aide, a proud declaration of parenthood to their neighbors. They were astonished to hear him declare that the Nairs were also his parents. In his short and sweet stay Rohan explored the depths of their lives. When they cried due to happiness, Rohan began to fear that their lives were getting too intimately knotted to be freed without an emotional breakdown. They felt as much: Mr Nair gently reminded his wife that releasing him from their cocooned existence was better than hand cuffing him, holding him a prisoner for their own selfish joys; who knows, if they set him free, Rohan might rush home to them, recollecting marvelous moments they had spent together. Besides, Mrs. Nair recalled from one of the casual conversations that Rohan would soon go abroad for higher studies. He would be gone tomorrow or two days later!

It was departure day. It came as suddenly and as unceremoniously as his arrival. Standing by the entrance of his room the Nairs were misty eyed, a little orphaned and solemn. Rohan could judge the rush of clouded emotions running through them, as the elderly couple could not control their pearly droplets trickling down, gushing now with full force unashamedly. They had come so close to Rohan; Mrs. Nair imagined he was their son in the last birth. To Rohan they were the closest he could find to his dream of ideal parents.

Rohan was packing his bags often fleeting glances at the Nairs; his heart skipped a beat as he mustered the grace to console and comfort the elderly couple; as they could feel their emptiness even more now, feel the time he regaled them with his cute antics and bountiful presence.

Spring time eluded them and now they could feel the heat stronger than before, when beads of sweat broke out on their foreheads, when all at once Rohan bowed down and touched their feet holding on to them till the Nairs lifted his head and each planted kisses on his forehead in turns, wishing this moment would last longer and in fact, be unending. Holding his palm they slipped in a gift envelope sealed with love. They blessed him and said "Son, you have made us feel so wanted, giving us the privilege of parenthood; even if it was for a short time, but the time spent was well spent. Please remember always, that we are both yours, and please do not hesitate to come back if you wish to; your magnanimous gestures, thoughts and actions will dwell in our hearts, till we breathe our last." Rohan was dumbfounded and clearing his throat said, "I had just come to attend a wedding, to spend one night here which was stretched to two full weeks under your parental care and love."

Rohan continued, "It is unthinkable that a couple like you would shower such love on a visitor like me, who is a guest this evening, gone tomorrow, to never come back again, as many guests are. Some couples shudder to imagine other's children as their own when from inside they would have a burning desire to have one of their own. Which makes you both saintly and your love paramount. I may have parents at home, friends and relatives everywhere, but you are jewels I would not part with for anything in the world. Through your anguish and loneliness, I could recognize that if you were given a chance, you both, Amma and Achan, would be better parents than my own biological parents. You have shown me through your inimitable affection that I feel the same pulse, the same heart beat like you, that we are destined to remain each other's, to reunite; to make hearts meet to play the symphony of love, vowing to always belong to each other, to make sure the candles are lit and kept burning unmindful of shower, wind or heavy rain."

CHAPTER 4

DESTINY'S FAVOURITE CHILD

"Man cannot remake himself himself without suffering. For he is both the marble and the sculptor."

Alexis Carrel

After my studies I had enough time on hand to pursue my hobby - provide tuitions at home, not for money, but to get satisfaction from imparting knowledge in a subject I was keen to teach. One bright sunny morning Rukma, our house helper, brought home her brother Ramu who was studying in the 8th grade. I opened the door to find a tall, lean, shy boy with wheatish complexion and magical twinkling eyes. He had pleasant manners and he looked at me as though he didn't want to impose himself on me. He was reserved and apologetic for seeking tuitions from me in Hindi. He was a hutment dweller with a well scrubbed face and a neat appearance and with a quietness rarely found today in boys of his age.

I had prided myself till then of my getting the highest marks in Hindi in the 10th grade but, as a teacher, realised that learning and writing were so different from teaching.

Ramu was a keen and a quick learner. The first day he promptly took down notes and answered my questions and then to my utter amazement, bent down to touch my feet. I told him it was unnecessary and urged him to address me as Didi rather than as Madam or Teacher. Rukma gave me the background to her request : Ramu had missed a year of his school due to ill health and repeatedly blamed himself for it, not the trying circumstances. He seemed always nervous and apprehensive, with fear lurking at the back of his mind about his health. Talking to him about his studies, his home and friends, I started to loosen his mind so that even my small efforts could help him to open up and assure him that it is normal to go through these testing periods, that these are learning experiences, stumbling blocks that can easily be removed with better understanding of oneself. I told him we are not sinners, we are makers of our destiny. Nothing can hurt us unless we allow ourselves to get hurt.

I didn't want to intrude into his sensitive past, so I waited for him to reveal the saga that caused him deep pain. One day he suddenly mumbled something and started speaking to me, unpretentious and sad, about how he lost a year and how he was ridiculed by his classmates, and even those were earlier considered close friends. He could not bear being reprimanded sternly by his teacher who had always talked about him as a potential star, a promising rank holder. It was as though a strong fierce storm blew over and shattered his dreams of gaining goodwill from everyone, to compete with himself and to prove to himself that all was not lost.

I had made out by then that Ramu was a self willed and fearless boy, with a reserve of confidence that he can muster when occasion demands it. He can excel and build his castle by the sweat of his brow. I told him" You are a firm believer in the Almighty, so loving, sensitive, with a wonderful character and discipline, nothing can stop you from achieving your goals. You are not to blame for what has happened. When we accept the hard knocks in our lives, a unique strength emanates from the inner enclaves of human wonder- strength that is yours and yours alone." I could feel him unburdening a weight off his shoulders when he used to speak to me. Gradually these conversations became an added responsibility. Not just to teach him but by doing so boost his confidence, understand him, encourage him so that he could pray to his Sun God, stand erect, fearless.

Some relationships have no name attached to them, no explanations to be given about, yet they mean a lot- the bonding between two persons irrespective of caste, creed and language barriers. There is an unspoken truth shared between two hearts working towards meeting each other. I was not trying to understand a person; I was waiting to see a budding aspirant flowering in front of me. I gave full credit to Ramu for mending the broken pieces of his life, for attempting to rediscover his potentialities without a murmur of self praise. He was looking more presentable now, taking an active interest in his life and work. I could note his burning desire to succeed. He studied with renewed vigour and concentration. In his first class test, he cleared the Hindi paper splendidly as even the other papers, way above my expectation. I was amazed by his drive, focus and commitment. Rukma gave me the news and I was thrilled.

The next day I waited for the tuition hour - to congratulate him. But that day he was absent... 2-3days had passed by, yet there was no trace of him or of Rukma who would come regularly with her Ramu. I soon started panicking - I hadn't known how much I would miss this habitual visit of the wonder kid smiling shyly, greeting me with a polite "namaste".

Days passed. I had begun missing Ramu who would share a cup of tea with me, nibbling at the cheese straw which was his favourite snack. Though he called me Didi, I felt a strong motherly affection for him, wanting to shelter him from baseless fears. I dreaded the thought that something may have gone wrong for him health wise or otherwise.

The dreaded thought returned the next day when the security guard rushed to our house and uttered the name Ramu. Ramu had been hospitalized. Late in the evening Rukma came pale and listless, to confirm the news. Ramu had a kidney problem and the doctors had advised that nothing short of a kidney transplant would work. Rukma said that they were short of money for the operation. I was Helpless: I didn't have the funds or the contacts to help him. I regretted not having the means to support him. She still thanked me for helping her brother with tuitions and even if it was a month or two, thought he was a changed person. Rukma's face suddenly lit up and said "Didi, please pray for us. That is more than enough for us. Some day Ramu and I can come back and Ramu can resume his studies with you." They had probably nothing to gain from this but a positive attitude could lead them to a safe pathway. Or so I hoped.

Hearing that he was battling with a life threatening illness, the stunned teachers from his school rallied to find a solution. It was not as hard to find a donor as it was to collect funds to pay the donor. As luck would have it, their search for a donor bore quick success. They contacted an NGO and through them a lady named Sama who instantly offered to help knowing the boy's background and the illness. Within a few days a kidney donor appeared through Sama's contacts, Pramil a middle aged Bengali. Now the question arose about the donation. It was decided that everyone of the school committee will help and the NGO will coordinate and get sponsorships. At such shaky periods the Almighty's mercy reigns supreme, residing in every member who believed in the human obligation to extend a helping hand, when we required several hands to unite - to give the young man the gift of a new life.

Ramu needed to make a comeback at least for those who had pinned their hopes on his success. On the day of his operation as he moved under sedation, on a stretcher to the operation theatre, Rukma and family bowed in deep prayer to the Almighty. Each one of them held a beaded chain and their fingers moved incessantly from one bead to the other.

The operation was over, all anxiously waited for the doctor. After an agonising wait, which seemed like ages, the doctor emerged. He seemed lost in thought. A few moments later, he held his palms in prayer to the Almighty and said all will be well. He asked everyone to silently pray for the boy. It was their faith that had saved a life. But all was not over. This was no ordinary operation and Ramu had to be kept under observation. He had to be kept away from others, from all possibility of infections. Rukma broke down and had to be carried away.

Ramu was recouping. It took many days but the doctor assured the family that he will do all he can and that their prayers will not go unanswered.

Days passed and Ramu came out of the hospital. The NGO and the school struggled but paid the bill. Ramu was now a winner and I thought, from now on there was no looking back. I was so grateful to the Almighty to present a new, confident Ramu who bounced back to a new beginning, a new birth. At one time he recollected how fortunate he was to be loved by his family and the people who had become to him a true extended family.

A week later, our bell rang ceremoniously one morning. I heard a familiar voice from outside. To my surprise it was Ramu and Rukma. The incarnation had rejuvenated his spirits. I prepared piping hot tea with tea masala the way he always liked. When he and Rukma got settled, Ramu spoke admirably well "The Almighty has given me a second chance, a life to prove my worth as I always wanted to. I can't thank everyone enough through words, but through my deeds I wish to create happiness and make you proud of me. Didi, I need your guidance and your good will much more now." I held his hands tightly to reassure him. At the end of each session I would relate stories of people who faced similar challenges. I said it would be the same with him. I hoped my conversations with him would have a therapeutic effect.

The final exams were fast approaching. The night prior to his exams, Ramu came promptly to seek my blessings. For the first time, I became more nervous than Ramu himself, I presumed. I requested him to light the lamp and burn the incense. While he was leaving, he turned his back with a look of reaffirmation and yet hidden anxiety.

During his exams and after he completed it, I didn't get an opportunity to see him.

More than two months passed. I sought Ramu's results. There was no sign of him. Rukma too had disappeared. One evening I walked through the narrow alleys to their hutment. The door had been locked. I asked the neighbors. They seemed to know very little about them. "Maloom Nahin was all I got. Do they know their village location or address? "maloom nahin". The weird silence baffled me and made me nervous. Finally one of them said, "wo gayaa, unka thabiyat". "Thabiyat? Kya huva" I asked. "maloom nahin. Ab wo nahin ayenge" was the answer. The May heat and my low blood pressure were acting on me and with this news I felt an acute pain in the legs. I could stand this no more. Hastily I returned home.

The results of Ramu's exams were declared after a couple of weeks. Long overdue, I thought. For Ramu it was a spectacular performance, the best in the class. One that called for a grand celebration.

Where was Ramu? My neighbor's maid told me that he had returned. I queued in front of his modest home where many had gathered to congratulate him. Because there was a special mention about him in the local language newspaper. He might even get a state scholarship!

I was told Ramu had gone to the hospital. The same hospital where he had his surgery! No he can't suffer any more. I rushed to the hospital. So did many of his school friends, his admirers and a few newspaper correspondents. I stood in the lounge with bated breath. Each moment seemed an eternity.

After a while I saw a frail figure coming out of the lift. From a distance Ramu spotted me and came straight to me. He hugged me and we wept unashamedly. I said, "There is peace and contentment today. I am so happy to experience the joy you feel from your accomplishment. Your success is the best gift for me; you're offering to a teacher the true reward. You have passed through the dark tunnels of uncertainty to capture the all pervading light which is not blinding, but engulfs you in its warmth, conjures up a timely glow, saying ever so loudly that there is life beyond excruciating suffering, peace beyond pain."

With Ramu was Dr Krishnappa, the doctor who had attended on him all along. This was a routine check up, but a necessary one. Krishnappa came up and said, "This boy will go very far. He is Destiny's Favorite Child!

Yes, indeed, Destiny's Favorite Child.

[The last heard from him came many years later - that he had joined an IT company. Ramu's is a classic example of a young man whom everyone would love to have as a son, as one who came back from the depths of no return. When he writes his story it will be true inspiration to innumerable students; they will know that there is the colorful rainbow beneath the dismal clouds. Today as I see Ramu in my son, struggling in a lesser-known college with vernacular studies I see the road less travelled, the road that brought an eternal blessing to Destiny's Favorite Child]

Chapter 5

BELA

"It isn't life that matters! 'Tis the courage you bring to it."

Hugh Walpole

There are stories that leave an indelible mark on our lives; stories of persons who are an asset to everyone but have to fend for themselves in dire circumstances. They want and do not get to be consoled with a comforting touch or kind word, that all will be well. Some do withstand tragic circumstances with fortitude. But all are not blessed with such good fortune.

Bela was in her late teens. Her father, Sashadhar Ghosh, owned an old building in Calcutta's Park Circus. They lived on the top floor, renting out the flats below. One flat was rented out to a group of malayali bachelors. Among them was Madhavan who was an Air force pilot. A handsome Brahmin in his late twenties. Madhavan was outgoing and had diverse interests: music, writing poetry, photography and of course travel. His small flat was a hub of innocent fun and frolic on weekends. Young job aspirants from his part of Kerala gravitated to Madhavan and his songs and stories.

Into this circle came fairly frequently Bela's brother, Shanker. Shanker too loved music. So did Bela whose music teacher was a frequent sight as he went up the stairs that led to Madhavan's room. Hearing Madhavan sing a strange Malayalam tune, Bela's teacher walked into Madhavan's room one evening. With Bela. He made Bela sing the same song that she did with amazing ease. Madhavan felt attracted to her, as he had never been to a girl. He thought of forgetting her- what? A Malayali brahmin and a schoolgirlish Bengali non-brahmin? No, that would never happen!

Yet Madhavan could not get her out of his mind. Little did he know that she too could not. Her teen aged budding romance blossomed and culminated in marriage soon after Madhavan proposed to her.

Both sets of parents were strongly opposed to the idea of their getting married but got reconciled to it after seeing them blissfully happy. The couple took a trip to Kerala where Bela delighted his parents by speaking or at least trying to speak in Malayalam.

Madhavan and Bela moved to a small flat in Ballygunge. Bela was a Bengali who learnt to cook malayali food, was a splendid cook and a perfect hostess and conversed in Malayalam fluently much to Madhavan's delight and pride. Madhavan lavished his love and praise on her and she received it all with a shy sweet smile of gratitude.

Their sacred bond produced three sprightly children, their three jewels as it were and they lived in a cozy nest of their own. It looked like nothing would disturb this union, this unity of family life. It seemed as though the Almighty had chosen an ideal couple to shower his worthiest blessings on them.

A long period of uninterrupted happiness is an extreme phenomenon and extreme pleasure often leads to extreme pain. The dancing demonic devil had risen from deep dungeons to destroy their peace with a vengeance. One morning Madhavan was unusually quiet not even sipping his piping hot coffee which Bela served him every morning with almost maternal care and love. She was clueless of what was to follow soon. Madhavan sat beside her and holding her close to him spoke of a dream he had: that in within a year he would pass away. Bela tried to pooh-pooh it but Madhavan believed in it as such things had happened to him and his mother. He called them premonitions. They looked so true to life. so real, so possible, he told her.

Bela didn't cry or speak; she was numb with unspoken fear. Madhavan spoke so seriously and tactfully that Bela was stumped and alarmed beyond imagination.

The next week saw him transferring his savings, investments, all in Bela's name, as though the countdown had started. To free himself from tension Madhavan took a trip to a few holy shrines and took his family on a holiday with him, when they ate, played and, gave themselves the most pleasurable time of their life -One last bash, he thought to himself. Bela looked on with utter disbelief at her husband's handsome face that showed no trace of melodrama or anxiety, living and loving the company of his dear ones, accepting each day as a precious gift.

One night his children snuggled unto him and Madhavan indulged in story telling while his children cuddled him, hugged him and planted sweet kisses on his cheeks. This was one time when he broke down in front of Bela. Bela too sobbed inconsolably, taking his hands in hers, in a fold of secrecy, wondering if it would be the last time she would look deep into his almond eyes-eyes that spoke volumes of his intense, lurking fear that she would not be able to manage without him.

These thoughts played havoc in his mind.

Then on a Monday morning when he relaxed to read the newspaper Madhavan had a telephone call. The pilot on duty had not turned up and he was urgently required to step in. Madhavan bid goodbye to his family and boarded the flight. - With some hesitation. What happened can be easily guessed but can one come to terms with it?

The phone rang incessantly, and by the time Bela lifted the receiver the damage had already occurred. The plane had crashed taking away many lives including Madhavan's. There was a tomb of grievance, but Bela had no time to mourn. She had to move forward, look ahead and raise her children aged 2, 5, 9.

Bela struggled but she brought up her children exactly the way her Madhavan would have liked, or so she imagined.

Bela's eldest son became a news editor in a leading newspaper, the daughter an architect and the younger son an ace model. Every one of them married and flew out of Bela's residence to their independent homes. Bela stared at her empty house, deserted and abandoned.

A year later, on a routine check up, Bela was diagnosed for breast cancer, The news of her illness was not as deafening as much as she felt disowned by her children. She was alone all through her treatment, through chemotherapy and radiation, barring one or two visits from her children. A visitor would have thought they were waiting to conduct the final rites on the funeral pyre.

A mockery of fate. Without expecting anything in return she at least had the satisfaction that her children were well placed in life. She didn't want to conquer death, but to face it bravely with prayers to accept death without suffering and without being a burden to anyone.

Just as the Durga Puja celebrations had started that year, Bela looked out and began counting the stars imagining Madhavan to be amongst the constellation. She realized that she had to leave this unwelcome "paradise" for a heavenly abode, Fortune was favoring her now. In her life she presented garlands of peace and tranquility to everyone but in death there was no one to place a wreath over her dead body. Bela was a woman of amazing zeal and substance on par with any man but she chose to be feminine and revelled in her femininity. Her death relieved her from pain and turmoil. She was victorious in death as in life. We've dreamt of heavenly goddesses, hut here was a lady noble and worthy, to be recognized and known as a goddess on earth, a manifestation of life's struggle and sacrifice.

CHAPTER 6

TEARS OF TRUE VICTORY

"We learn as much from sorrow as from joy, as much from illness as from health, from handicap as from advantage, and indeed perhaps more."

Pearl S Buck

It looks as if it all happened a long time ago. We had just moved into our new home in Pune. We had great difficulty in getting a maid, maybe due to our high expectations and general mistrust of maids, may be unavailability of maids, or just that they were too expensive. We thought of a maid as our housekeeper, more as a family member than as a maid.

The next morning, the door bell rang frantically and resonantly to wake us up. I opened it to find a lean, tall, lady outside the door swaying her body to and fro, with a mischievous glint in her twinkling eyes, adjusting demurely her nine yard saree. I was stunned hearing her endless chatter in between her giggles and prattle. She looked attractive in a strange way. I thought she would be a source of great amusement and liveliness. Wouldn't she get breathless talking so vociferously and animatedly, I wondered.

In all this animated, giggly conversation, I sensed a hidden sadness although it never came in the way of her movements and actions. She sounded sincere and committed, and was promptly appointed the lady in charge of our home and hearth. She was eager to please and would spring to action whenever anyone of us needed assistance. Kalpana was now an important part of our lives, working at odd hours, cooking special meals, shorteats, snacks and sweets with rare excitement. I began depending on her more than I had on others in the past. To show my appreciation and indeed affection, I presented her one day an expensive gift. She reacted by throwing up her hands, "If some day mam you get upset with me and accuse me of stealing this gift, I'll feel betrayed and deceived"!

As the days sped by my fondness for her increased by volumes. But she had begun to be silent, unapproachable. There was a sense of boredom, a visible monotony on her face, but she continued doing her duties as well as she had done, without any bickering or grumbling. I had to know her better : something was holding her back, may be she did not trust me to open up her mind and heart. One afternoon, as I got up after a short nap I heard a long, unceasing wail. I went down to see Kalpana seated on the floor, below the staircase, crying like a child. She cried, covering her head with her palms. She was a picture of misery. She said she was defeated by life, her husband was critically ill, in the hospital with a terminal disease. She now had to support her ailing husband and raise her two growing school going children. She could not think of any immediate step to save her from being penniless, as the hospital bills were exorbitant and she would have had to work much harder to make both ends meet. I tried to console her and promised to do what my husband, away in the Middle East, and I could do but her grief was inconsolaable.

The next day, I asked Kalpana to bring any medical records her husband had. We had them examined by a friend, a medical doctor. The condition was indeed grave with no hope of recovery. The doctor told us privately that he had serious liver and kidney problems. I could not tell Kalpana all this but tried to help her. I also said she could take a few days off and adjust the timings to take care of the home and the husband.

Kalpana would not hear of this. Barring occasional delays she would come and finish her work fast. A few days later she came back and said the husband had come home and there was slight improvement in his health. Confined to bed and in pain, he kept reassuring her that he was fine and that she should concentrate on her health and their children, their joy and pride. In normal health he would often surprise her with a few roses or a box of sweets. He would bring multicoloured glass bangles and carefully put them through her delicate hands. Nostalgia pained her now and brought tears into her eyes. Her priority now was to ease his pain both physically and mentally.

Life was cruel to her, but she had no complaints; she braved the storm with indescribable maturity, without exhibiting her suffering to anyone. As the husband's condition worsened, Kalpana took leave of us to devote her time to him and the family. I still do not know how she managed her finances- may be she sold the only piece of land she had back in her village, may be she borrowed from her brother. We gave whatever help we could.

And then the cutain fell suddenly one morning. Kalpana sent a short message through a maid we had hired. Her husband closed his eyes to this world of pain and suffering, but creating a vaccum in her life.

Kalpana came to resume work after a fortnight. She was devastated by his tragic death, lonely, in a stony silence. My husband offered to finance her childrens' education and urged them to study well despite the loss and bought the school books. They kept their word-they had the second or third rank in class- but Kalpana was reticent to take any help for more than the first year. She started working in several places and earning enough to cover their education.

We left Pune a few months later. During my visits to Pune once a quarter she would meet me and bring for us home cooked breakfast, lunch and dinner.

Kalpana came one day looking refreshed and vibrant wearing a bright red and blue saree. Knowing that I was observing her colourful saree she said, "I feel my husband's presence and warmth even today. Why should I stop living even if he is not physically present? I am determined to live and educate my children, as he wanted me to, to bring back the happiness which they sadly missed so that they grow up worshipping their father rather than mourning his death. I'll shower all my love on them. This will be my undying mission from now on."

True to her words of courage, today her daughter is independent having completed her M.Com and her son is working in a factory. Kalpana has a bank account. As she is a cook par excellence, she supplies home meals to the neighbouring houses on a regular monthly basis. Persons living in neighbouring colonies flock to her dwelling to get a treat of her delicacies. To me she represents an ideal wife and an ideal mother, a person with high self-esteem.

From the gloom of a dark, cloudy night she moved into the sunshine of a new existence., Success was a well deserved reminder of her toil and sacrifice. Life was deceiving, disappointing, but she smelt its sweet fragrance and buried the thorns.; the daisies were separated from the dying plants. Today she is truly victorious, a celebrity in her own circle. There comes a luminous light, calling for long, thunderous applause.

SECTION II

LABOUR OF LOVE

Chapter 7

Bountiful Joy

"A miracle is really the only way to describe motherhood and giving birth. It is unbelievable how God has made us women and babies to endure and be able to do so much. A miracle indeed. Such an incredible blessing."

Jennie Finch

What seemed like an unending nine months of carrying a baby in my womb, which I so desired, ended when I heard the first cry like a calling bell to greet me, to reveal that a parcel, a part of me has been delivered. As I gently opened my eyes to catch a glimpse of my newborn baby, a whole new world unfolded itself in front of me, a creation so magical that needed my undivided attention and care. All at once this adorable baby captivated me, staring astonishingly at me; his twinkling button eyes sweetly studied me; and soon retired for a good sleep after his first exercise, his introduction to his mother, -who was now the center of his universe, his existence. Motherhood to me is an extension of me, giving me my own flesh and blood, someone I can call my own. The birth of my miracle baby represents the purest of joys, and his innocent love to me -a mother who lives to capture her baby's happy growing years. I looked upon the years as a route to gauge my own growth and strengths.

When my baby cried, I cried too; when he was happy I was overjoyed. This was the sacred bond we shared with each other. He was considerate to grant me peace and quiet even at a tender age when he was expected to cry or moan for his food, needs and comforts. The trauma, the pain of labor was replaced by ecstasy and gratitude, the moment my longing eyes searched for my baby --who needed me as much as I needed him!

As my baby grew into a child, I learnt and -still learn -a lot from him, by observing, watching and understanding him. Instead of bargaining for love, he was keen to present me with plentiful love, not expecting anything in return. Without blaming or taunting me, he has accepted me with my flaws and weaknesses. I realize that this is his unconditional love for me, removing any barrier that may come between us. So touched am I each time when my son from the bottom of his heart says, "Amma your presence means more to me than anything else." I am moved to tears when he says my sheer existence gives him a reason to live, a purpose in life.

My indisposition separated us from each other, sending him to a country, which was alien to him, at a time when we needed each other most. With deep anguish, my dearest son bore the separation with stoic courage and commendable maturity and responsibility. To stay away from the mother whom he loved so dearly was an irreparable loss for him, when he needed me to touch him, console him. I longed to reassure him by saying "forgive me, my son, I am torn away from you out of compulsion than choice." Every time I heard his mournful voice I was choked with emotion, missing him very much. Yet I continued to receive week after week tender messages stating –"Amma, I love you, don't worry everything will be alright"

He didn't expect to be brought home soon. Though very shattered, he would ask me if he could rest his head on my lap when he comes home to me someday. This would question me of my hopeless existence, as I was uncertain of being present with him ever so often again. My only prayer, my desperation was to look on to my beloved son's growth in a happy and healthy surrounding free from the shackles of tension, worries and instability.

It is due to our Creator's blessings that my darling son and I are back together in each other's arms, valuing each other's presence more than ever before. Every step I take, my son helps me to put forward an extra step so that I live and enjoy the present and happily wait for a prosperous future. My son, you may travel a long distance to where life takes you, but you will still be tied to my umbilical cord all my life. Thank-you for teaching me that there are people other than you to take care of. I live for you but you will be happier if I spread my love to everyone as well. The selfless love we share now brings an interdependency, attachment and belongingness.

It is your persistent love, which has united us by divine grace and power. The most precious reward I receive is when you say "Amma you are the best mother in the world." Rejoicing in this offering of true joyful experience I feel like a complete mother, a complete woman.

CHAPTER 8

TILL THE END OF TIME

"A great marriage is not when the perfect couple comes together. It is when an imperfect couple learn to enjoy their differences."

Dave Meure

Predictions sometimes open up unpredictably in our favour and make our dreams come true. Marriage was evading me, so I believed. I was a young bride-in –waiting, waiting and hoping for an eligible bachelor of my choice, a few years elder, who would sweep me off my feet, the die-hard romantic that I was -and still am. I was 24, unmarried, ready to take the plunge and in my priority list, marriage was priority 1 – to pave the way for a home built on love, trust, companionship and friendship.

Friends of mine were sending messages of their moving happily to the "married" status. I too wished to own a love nest. You can imagine the rising well of anxiety inside an Indian girl, in a coventional family setting, as she moves from 21 to 22, them 23 and 24 with the family receiving no marriage proposals, waiting for some divine intervention to make things happen!

Nothing seemed to happen. Just then, outside a temple we visited in Bombay, an astrologer looked at my horoscope and predicted that within a fortnight, by end of May "92, I would receive a proposal for matrimony and tie the ceremonial knot before 12th September the same year. As luck would have it, the proposal came within a fortnight through an uncle of my father and and with amazing speed, not only was the marriage fixed but preparations began for the event. I was given in hand for marriage on 10th September. I thought of the astrologer as a heavenly messiah, blessing me with marriage, something that had forsaken me.

Two days prior to our wedding, in walked the man of my life through the corridors of Anand Hall to the corridors of my mind and then into my life -like a god's gift of goodness. His gentle persona, kind eyes, and soulful voice attracted me instantly towards him. There were his family members present and so were mine. An embarrassing situation for some, but for me it was an ecstatic moment when romanticism got the better of me to elevate me into a higher plane and with lightning speed he placed a ring into my quivering finger. I was stunned by his courage and remained speechless.

I had just recovered from typhoid and been advised a fair amount of rest and care about the about the food and drinks that I took. I was weak and could barely balance myself on my two feet. There were only two days more for our marriage. My new anchor and would be life partner fed me with piping hot drinks and food supplements that I had not even thought of. And on the day of our wedding, he took my hand in his to solemnize our marriage by circling the seven rounds of the holy fire.

I valued marriage as a sacred bond between two people, a union of two family backgrounds and culture.

A month after our wedding we flew to a foreign land, my new settlement so I perceived. Feeling awkward, surrounded by people who barely had any resemblance to anyone I had known, made me featherless, homeless and abandoned, residing in a strange land with stranger inhabitants.

All my fears were put to rest, when even in a large gathering amidst noise and chaos, he spotted me easily while his searching eyes followed me to shelter me. I noticed that he encouraged people to love me just the way he cared for me. So amused was I observing my husband mingling with his friends and relatives with a sense of belonging, selflessly loving them without a thought of his own personal needs or luxuries. From one glimpse of this amazingly thoughtful person, I knew that this kind heart would bring a complete change in my life, uplifting me from leading an uneventful life to something exceptional, prompting me to sway to the tune of joyous laughter, in a mood of festivity.

When I conceived our baby, the news exhilarated us and we took it with nervous anticipation. He would often come up with "I hope nothing will happen to you when you are in labour. If it does, how will I live without you? You must live for me and live with me."

Raising a candle and praying that all will go well for me, he had more faith in my recovery than I had for myself. We were, for long, separated by distance, he in the Middle East and I in India. But distance brought us closer, and each time we met, we spent our days creating exceptional opportunities to please each other, to rekindle our relationship with a new urge to lengthen the period of unitedness than to indulge in frivolous quarrels.

There were times when, due to my indisposition, I began demanding attention and my husband gave me emotional support. I realised that he had an in-born ability to do this:, everyone who has benefitted from him emotionally, physically or financially, compliments him and thanks him for taking him to the thresholds of success. Essaying a life of service without expecting even an acknowledgment, he is so special and supportive and earns lasting friendships. I believe, this simple, honest unassuming man is a boon, a saviour whom I worship. So thankful am I to the Eternal Giver for introducing me to this picture of peace and harmony. He says, and I echo it with all my conviction today, that after every dark night there is a bright day ; that nothing can be worse than what we have already experienced ; that good times are ahead for us with occasional ups and downs.

The beauty of our relationship is often felt through the language of silence; we communicate through unspoken words. Today that unspoken silence means everything to us.

Sacred Bonds

I am fortunate to have you
Someone I can call my own,
Destiny has brought us together
Divided by distance
We are happy to be one
What lasts forever
Is not the pain we show
But the glee and glow
In a communion of souls
What is mine is ours now
How I'd love to grow with you,
Holding your hand
Till the end of time.

Chapter 9

Home Coming

Many years have passed, but my memory remains strong of the first time I touched the feet of my father-in- law, with reverence, as he looked on with the warmest of paternal love and affection. He tenderly held my hands to indicate that my place was in his heart and not at his feet. All he wished was to accept me as his daughter without expecting anything in return, monetary or otherwise. As I got to know him better, I began to look up to him as a father more than as a father-in-law.

Many mistook my father-in -law to be a strict, forbidding, figure. But to me he was an exemplary figure who could give strength to others by showing how turbulence can be faced with utter poise and tranquility. One who always gave me a reason to smile!

We used to journey together, taking rounds of visits to his relatives' places, whenever I appeared forlorn or upset, as my husband was away in the Middle East. I was charmed by his culinary expertise, which gave us delightful dishes, delicacies to capture my smile, to cheer me up when I was sad. To my surprise he used to serve me food with utmost care and concern.

For a man who could himself be stormy, he often witnessed the erratic mood swings in me, with complete silence and understanding, without complaining one bit or accusing me for the temper I exhibited during unpredictable states. Calming me, he would say "You are completely alright. This turbulence is a passing phase. We love you and will take good care of you. You are my little child, a good human being, I wish you the very best always."

What more would I want from a gentleman who gained comfort by understanding, solace by giving solace. I felt safe, secure and strong in his majestic presence. He had a king size personality and was a great person himself.

He was a wealthy man and when occasion arose, he freely shared his riches with the needy, who in turn prayed for his good health and cheer. When we, the entire family would visit him, he would greet us with a grand reception, with a luxurious spread of the choicest food, presented in a stylish and splendid way. Particular of every detail, he took special interest in our welfare, our wellbeing.

Missing his wife's holy presence, he would have post- lunch story sessions with us which were a memorable flashback to the treasured moments he spent with his woman who could read his thoughts and words. A very passionate good soul, he was also emotional ; he was moved to tears with a single affectionate word -something he craved for. His tough exterior was a mask to prevent himself from getting close to anyone --so that he refrained from getting hurt or felt let down by people.

I thought I would be fortunate to direct him through our doorstep into our hearts forever. One year before his sad demise, he disclosed to me, with a mischievous glint in his eyes, of an astrologer's predictions: that, within a year he would leave this earth and embrace death, or live another fifteen years, cherishing his freedom and liberty. I did not take this seriously. But the call came within a year.

Here was a man who had loved and lived life to the fullest! I was devastated by his predictable death which I found very difficult to recover from.

Two years later, I revisited my father-in law's home. I could still feel his presence, though amidst gathered dust, the house was no more a home- a barren house, with overgrown elderly plants and trees all mourning his death. My eyes turned misty, suddenly overcome with the realization that he had passed away; uncontrollable tears trickled down my cheeks. His photographs smiled at me but the majestic presence of a man of discipline and control was missing. Just before he shut his eyes to this world, he declared pointing to the sky, that his late faithful wife, his life partner was beckoning to him to join hands with her forever.

I salute you Achan (father) for teaching me that I may be all alone but not lonely. I am grateful to you for showing me that respect is earned and not given on a platter and that there are men who prove superbly that these are still the days of magnanimity.

CHAPTER 10

A DAY IN THE LIFE OF AN ETERNAL OPTIMIST

There are enchanting days that I wish would last longer than 24 hours. I remember one in July 2006, shortly after my birthday… serving my father with a couple of dishes which were his favourites. He and I spent a good two hours together in what seemed an interminable evening of mirth and laughter. As always, he was appreciative and he affectionately blessed me and retired to bed with a sense of contentment and relaxation never seen before. Totally clueless of the chain of events that the next day-the inauspicious26 July- would bring.

It was a ghastly morning. Nature's fury knew no bounds. The rains had started early morning, though as a drizzle, but gathering clouds thickened by the afternoon making the sky appear dark and frightening. Gripped with an unknown fear, I had a premonition that something terrifying was going to happen, the thought itself threatened the peace of our quiet home all of a sudden. I consoled myself with the feeble thought that it will not last although the power packed rains poured heavily and showed no signs of abating.

Fortunately, my mother and I were indoors in the safety of our home. To our horror, my father was beyond reach and security at the other end of Bombay, in Churchgate, a considerable distance from our home. He was to speak at a seminar and then catch a train in the evening for Vapi, Gujarat. By 3p.m., the roads were heavily flooded and we were warned by television channels not to venture out. It was a disturbing sight: vehicles dashing through the flooded roads, several breakdowns, wastes, dead animals and garbage all being swept by the floods and mass hysteria while people were rushing desperately to reach their respective homes. In some buildings the lower floors were submerged in the waters, furniture and electronic gadgets were floating and the impending tragedy threatened to take a big toll of human lives.

There was no news from my father in all this chaos and disorder. When the phone rang last, he said he was forced to rest in an immobile cab -that could no longer move because of the rising level of rain water. Shattering his hopes of getting back to the comfort of our home. After which there was silence from his end. News came trickling that one in Bandra and another in Ghatkopar was sucked into the open manhole. Bits and pieces of news, were being carried by the channels. None wasencouraging, none spoke of the water receding. The city was under siege.

My mother and I panicked, moaned and cried in despair. We were overcome with unbearable fears that perhaps we may never see him again. Why couldn't all the days be as bright and promising as the previous day when serenity and even silence was reassuring?. By then we were alarmed at the thought of how my father was spending hours without food and water and how much his knee problem would have added to his miserable immobility. We heard from our neighbours that college boys and girls were distributing food packets to stranded travellers and hoped these would reach my father.

At around 5 pm we heard that trains had stopped in their tracks and many had been cancelled. At around 7pm, the lights went off in our building, outside and in the far distance. Throughout Bombay. We were not prepared for this. We didn't have even a single candle at home. Slowly my mother searched for a matchbox with the help of my mobile phone and lit up a lamp that lay in the dining room. We both sat in a corner as we imagined the horror that my father must have been facing. We prayed profusely not being able to bear the suspense and the mystery.

Just then, our neighbour- three floors up- Mrs. Gracy knocked at our door frantically as all members of her family had been caught in the massive downpour near the railway station in Andheri. They were not too far and were yet cut off and would not return for the night. Mrs Gracy was terrified. She was all alone and wanted me to help her by spending the night at her flat. She pleaded with me and my mother, even though, she said, she knew my mother would be all by herself. My kind mother said she empathized with her plight and asked me to accompany her to her home. With a brave face my mother patted my shoulder saying, "Give her all the strength and courage she requires. I'll be fine. Right now she needs you more. It is God's will, and I have faith in God". She could pacify me with these words but I wondered who would console her ; she would cry perhaps the whole night for the safety of her husband.

At the break of dawn, as the water started receding, Mrs, Gracy's husband returned, all exhausted. A friend, Mr Chatterjee, who had addressed the seminar along with my father also reached home at 10 am. Seeing people streaming in to their homes only added to our sense of panic: there was no trace of my father. A group of social volunteers just then came into the building to enquire whether anyone was missing. We thought of the worst possible things that may have occurred. An epitome of patience and tolerance, my father was an eternal optimist; his sole purpose seemed to be to see us happy, loved and entertained, to see us smiling, to see that not even a drop of tear ever fell over my eyes. All we ever wanted was to get back my dear father safe and sound. He was and is dearer to us than our own lives. This was one of the many times I truly valued and respected his holy presence in my life – his guiding me, moulding me, watching every step I took, making my life worthwhile, promising me that better days will always come to me.

We waited and as the water receded, so did our hopes of getting him back. Around 2.30 p.m we heard a shout and a loud knock at our door. It was our neighbour's son. The knock was loud and reverberating. I bent down on my knees to pray for that ray of hope which was evading us till now. The shout and the knock persisted. The boy cried out "Open, Open, Uncle has come!" I could wait no longer. I peeped through the kitchen window to find the tall robust figure with a cherubic, young face waving to us with a tired, frail smile. It was unmistakably my Papa. I only wanted my father beside me. Nothing else mattered. My father showed no traces of disgust or displeasure, not even complaining of any pain or discomfort. He was like a wounded soldier who walked miles with his head held high.

I felt as though all the musical instruments that I knew were orchestrating to play a sweet melody unknown and unheard, and the strumming and the drumming were rising to a crescendo!

26th July 2006 was a disaster. 27th was a rebirth. We celebrated our reunion with gratitude and gaiety : gratitude to God for gifting back my father, and gaiety over the rebirth.

Today, I feel that gratitude all over again for his crossing a well lived and well spent 83 yrs. I am fortunate to be blessed with a magnanimous father who is a father anyone could ask for in this lifetime.

Chapter 11

The Queen of Hearts

"If your heart is pure, then all things in your world are pure."

Ryokan

IT was an extraordinary day as I stood in my balcony knowing not what to do. Observing the sun mischievously peeping through the pregnant clouds, I glanced at a matchless black, white and yellow striped bird blissfully perched on a nearby tree whose leaves remained still and unturned. The beauty of nature in all its bloom, witnessed the quiet, watchful bird suddenly flapping its colourful wings and freely flying high in gay abandon and wishful playing.

I then spotted a ferocious looking dog climbing the slope facing our verandah swiftly shaking its tail making the empty space his own private territory. I took a quick liking to this member from the barking club, though from a safe distance. As I was slowly turning around to my world of nothingness, I was overwhelmed, by a strikingly beautiful lady, sweetly waving at me, of whom I knew nothing, but all at once craved to know more.

Her gentle outstretched arms wanted to reach out to me. The more I responded to her friendly invitations, the more I was drawn to her angelic smile and child like innocence. A rush of undiluted emotion swept all over me, waiting to reciprocate her love and affection like dew drops resting on thirsty petals thirsting for many more drops to occupy a sea of humanity.

The next day as I was awaiting the car to drive in, I was captivated by the winsome face, the same adorable figure ushering me towards her, longing to be noticed, attended and recognized. Her feather touch, her soft delicate fingers feeling me, in hushed tones, she revealed her name "Sowmya", a name which suits her calm and serene nature.

I felt a deep sense of attachment to this lovely lady as she conversed intelligently, making fond sincere enquires about me, my family, our well-being. What struck a chord in my heart was, when each time she spoke to me, it brought out the best sentiment in me, urging me to be part of her inner joy, her unspoilt simplicity and the purity of a fascinating, intuitive mind. A mind reading through my restlessness, circling me into her motherly shelter of calm and peace.

I realized empathy had a significant role in binding us together. I thought of Sowmy's challenging life which didn't exhibit a trace of envy. She is the chosen one, happy with the simple pleasures of life.

Sometimes I wonder is Sowmya real? How can she be so gracious and composed in cold adversities of life? She is so different from my intolerant self. Her special quality is her uncomplaining nature -not expecting to pluck the bright roses from other peoples garden to make them her own, not living on borrowed happiness.

Appreciative glances were coming her way as I marveled at her exclusive choice of a traditional saree draped carefully, elegantly around her slim poised frame -and the matching 'pottu' on her forehead with her natural radiance. She looked alive and spectacular, resembling a Bengali picturisation of a Goddess. As I watched her from a distance, I could picture her as a person with admirable strength, perseverance and determination.

Countless days are passing by quickly. Soon Sowmya, the Queen of hearts will be leaving us to be back to her home, the culture and comfort she is familiar with. I'll miss you, dear Sowmya but instead of bidding a tearful goodbye, I'll always be grateful to you for showing me a path to brave all odds with a reassuring smile. I pray for your happiness always. You are the angel I love, for what you are than what you do or don't, you are Ananya (the incomparable) who will tide over the toughest of battles, emerging a winner, a reigning Queen of hearts, my idol, my inspiration. Our abode will remember this exquisite lady with a golden heart whose sweet memories I'll treasure for many more years to come

CHAPTER 12

A HOME AWAY FROM HOME

"I slept and dreamed that life was joy
I awoke and found that life was service
I acted, and behold, service was joy."

Rabindranath Tagore

There is a saying 'Athithi Devo Bhava' which means the guest is God. Indian are believed to be excellent hosts who consider it a huge honour to have guests in their home and go out of the way to please them. Home Stay is therefore a concept that many Indians readily accept. Guests are accomodated in the family home or in separate quarters nearby and in some provided as much comfort as in a reputable hotel.

I am accustomed to a clean environment at home and to the absence of creepy, crawling wanderers, seen all over in some holiday homes. These are otherwise attractive- open with lush green fields, overgrown trees, heartwarming greenery with scenic surroundings, stunning landscapes and thickly carpeted green hills. I have a constant fear that these attract fine and huge creatures intruding privacy to my astonishment and woe. I fear that these species would enter my glass of water or crawl onto my bed. I have been nursing this phobia from quite awhile; though to others it may seem baseless, to me it is at once petrifying and justified.

All my fears were put to rest when we sashayed our way into The Chateau home stay in Coorg. The gate opened just as we arrived; to greet us was a warm energetic lady with an infectious smile, with a close cropped hair, looking radiant and winsome. We were ushered into her home, and my eyes dodged to see if I could spot any of the endangering species. To my surprise, this anscestral home was spotlessly clean, well furnished, with a homely decor, intricately carved wooden furniture, all so authentic and fascinating. A working chiming grand father clock would alert me to wake up to a welcoming cool ambience, with excellent food hosted by the family which was a deliciously traditional Coorgi cuisine. The Chateau was a perfect place to stay with easy access to the city market through the tapering, gliding slopes leading into a sparkling circle of life It was ideal for a secluded, tranquil holiday. Once we reached the home, we were again inhaling a magnificent view of nature, soothing sounds of birds, a calm and serene atmosphere. It was one of the gorgeous holiday homes with an alluring charm and character.

This home stay belonged to Mrs. Sagari and her family. On arrival she promptly served us piping hot flavoured tea which was refreshing. It relieved us of our tiredness from our exciting, safe journey. Sagari was gracious, particular about the minutest detail that would make us happy, anxious to see that all our needs were met with astute keenness and expertise. During my stay in this home, it was unfortunate that I was ill; I did not sink into desperately low spirits only because of Sagari and her family, who were soon developing us into a larger family of her own. Sagari mirrored my discomfort as I held my stomach with griping pain, when she folded my hand to hold a cup of warm water and pass it into my quivering hands. She knew that was the only thing I could have had that day; that touched a chord in my heart beyond imagination, the hot water was as holy as Amrut and the bubbling hot rice gruel she prepared just for me was curing me of my ailment even further. Till then I was drowning in deep despair. Sagari dear livened the atmosphere and lifted my spirits with her comforting words, actions and gestures.

Sagari's children were standing examples of being well brought up, well mannered and lovable. There was a unique, strange chemistry between us, an extraordinary need to belong to each other, never to part, a craving to stay in this splendid home amongst these luminaries who were unknowns but were bonding with us so well. It cemented a beautiful relationship that could last a life time ; I hoped that we would meet again, cherish many more such brilliant moments. Sagari's home stay was less a house and more of a home. As we posed for photographs my eyes turned moist, as Sagari in all her beauty and glory bid us goodbye and we drove down the slope, waving inconsolably.

This kept my mind ticking. I thought that women like Sagari were at once enterprising and home oriented and coud strike a fine balance between the role of a home maker and that of an effective business entrepreneur. They are not only committed and dutibound but go beyond duty to strive for providing their Athithi luxury, pleasure, rest and health without concentrating purely on self gain and self satisfaction. I remember the times at The Chateau where I would wake up to the freshest of mornings into this blessed abode, and I would instantly decide that if were to visit Coorg again I'd be thrilled beyond words to be happily staying with Sagari because she represented a picture of a perfect host, to appear, breezing into our lives, to envelope us in her cozy home, a home away from home, a little heaven perched on a solemn hilltop. Some images flit through the mind, some endure, some linger to become the best experiences we have ever had in this lifetime. Our short and sweet association with The Chateau and its humble family is one of them, to remind me that there's always a heart to give and a will to please if there is an eager recipient to accept it and appreciate it.

Chapter 13

A School to Remember

School days bring back sweet memories ; my personality began taking shape and I was being moulded into one who must face the world with dignity and honour. I was fortunate to join a prestigious convent school at one corner of a narrow lane in Pali Hill, away from th bustle of activities all around the hill.

The school routine started with the assembly and soon after, an inspection to oversee personal cleanliness, -our nails, hair styling, and shoes. My second standard teacher, Mrs Williams, was strict but kind. Knowing that I had just entered school, she tried to be strict and firm with me but changed her mind watching me shiver at the very sight of her. Perhaps to overcome this fear, she appointed me the Prefect of the class. Everyday I had to pray aloud till the sound was deafening, sing a hymn melodiously and Praise the Lord, almost dramatically :each time I enacted I was rewarded a toffee. The toffee was a trophy for me, made my day special. I ventured out to perfect the ritualistic performance; gradually I bettered the performance ; the toffees multiplied as my devotion increased.

Mrs. Williams taught me to respect my duties however small they were. She holds a special place in my heart as she made me treat every work as a work of art, and to do it with utmost sincerity, to the best of my ability.

The most colourful of our teachers was our Marathi and Hindi teacher, two in one, who added a unique flavour and spice to my life. She was a prosperous looking lady. However threatening she wished to be, her anger was not taken seriously by us. She had passed her prime, was romantic to the hilt and yet unmarried. She would feed us with tales of many eligible bachelors proposing to her and married men making a beeline for her company. In between uncontrollable giggles and controlled laughter, we would put innocent queries to hear more of her favourite stories –to fill up nearly half the time allotted to that class. She would blush, and play with her thin strands of hair. We were dumbfounded when she came up with expressions like "lizards are reptiling on the walls," and "No shame to you." We had memorized these lines so well, that well before she pouted the, we whispered them to each other. Yet, she was fond of me and I was fond of Hindi which she taught. I am ever so grateful to her for motivating me and giving me fair opportunities to showcase my dancing skills, which I was so passionate about. A true sport, for our Children's day special function she plaited her hair complete with colourful ribbons, wore our school uniform with a red tie and held her palms close to sing a hindi song of a yesteryear's film. Much to the amusement of her colleagues and embarassment of the nuns she began crooning at a high pitch crooning and cooing like a cute overgrown baby.

At our annual Alumni Meet last year, I learnt with deep regret that she had passed away some years ago in her sleep -as she always wanted to. She had said once in the class, with great conviction, that a fairy goddess in her protective care would take her to heaven... Some people will always live in our hearts and minds. They educate and also entertain but within themselves live unfortunate lives, barely rising above an oppressive sense of misery...till a fairy goddess comes and takes them away!

Moving on to the higher classes, I grew to admire most of my teachers, nuns and staff who painstakingly taught us discipline, as they dedicated their lives to matching qualities of patience and tolerance, which were not just taught but practised by them.

We eagerly looked forward to our yearly school fest when, in the food stalls, delectable sweets and snacks were displayed for all to see and savour. Food lovers amongst us—most were-would queue up in dozens for items that gave a true flavour of India —brought essentially by parents. The stalls were run by us, the children who, in the bargain, pocketed the money from the sales.

I was fortunate to get a good conduct certificate almost every year. Nervous to the extreme, I walked the path to the stage, trying to look gracious, decent and obedient as a badge of good conduct was being attached to my name. Whenever my prize was announced I heard some hoots, huge cries and whistling, I guess, from my friends. Was that an applause of congratulation or an expression of amusement, I wondered.

At the PTA a parent suggested that movies could be screened every month for us students, who were starved of entertainment. Our school peon was the leading man to do the honours of adjusting and rearranging the film to project the movie from a pre-historic projector on to an empty wall in front of us. The pictures were mostly blurred images; the location was our school garage. So dark was it inside that we would lazily lean on each other and our minds could reach our dreamland while the movie dragged on. Our peon was sternly instructed to switch off the projector during intimate scenes : they should not corrupt innocent minds.

The Farewell Day arrived at the end of our 10th grade. It was an occcasion of parting with many, a moment of emotional upheaval for me. Will we meet again or be lost among the multitudes? We started talking of future plans and of many happy moments we had shared because of and at the school. We were told that a sumptuous meal was awaiting us! There was no sign of the caterers ; as we were kept wondering, our class teacher appeared: she had taken on the whole responsibility by turning into a super chef for the evening. Her home-. made meal was superb. More touching was her thoughtful gesture that left us weeping and speechless; we thanked her immensely for her love and its beautiful expression. I was overcome with extreme sadness and left the school with a heavy heart. The nun who cried the most was the one who had reprimanded me harshly once in the lower class when I kept mum and failed to answer her question. It was a time to forgive and forget. I preferred to remember the good days I had spent in the affectionate unity of school life- with teachers, nuns, friends, peons and nannies.

The grounding I got in my school days has made me learn that I needed to live and love everyone regardless of their skin, colour, caste religion or culture. "All are one, we are the children of God "-these words of wisdom still linger in my mind. We need to walk a mile for every gain that comes our way, nothing comes easy. If happiness were all pervading and permanent, we would have hardly valued it. Often in grief we value happiness and in happiness we thank God. Education at my school was for me a primary need for my all round development and steady growth. The thought that lay embedded in my mind was; what is not yours, was never there, the dark days are reminders of happier days gone by; to conjure up good fortune and better days ahead!

SECTION III

HOPES FOR ANOTHER DAY

Chapter 14

Compassion not for Humans Alone

"See the world as your self. Have faith in the way things are Love the world as your self; then you can care for all things."

Lao Tse

There was a time when I used to feast on animal flesh - still warm after the inhuman slaughter which I used to just miss seeing. It used to be cooked with spice mixes and juice extracts from tomatoes, onion pastes and then spice pastes to garnish. It was then presented as an exotic dish at an exclusive spot on the dining table. I fed myself with meat and fish, with all that was considered edible meat with lip smacking relish and with sadistic pleasure. I did not have any regrets then in thinking that beastly attacks were practiced on harmless animals like cows and goats which freely grazed in our lands almost as our companions, that they were tortured and brutally chopped into chunks and minced on the cutting edge to satisfy our palates.

One day prior to the killing of a helpless, homeless goat, it was tied firmly to the bars of a railing. It had been fed to an enormous size which made it look well fed and healthy. It was tied and was searching for release, bleating nervously for freedom.

Through the grills of our windows, I could hear the agonising screeching and shouting of the caged animal. My heart beat anxiously when I spotted a hefty man, who looked monstrous and demoniac, lifting a deadly weapon to an height and bringing it down heavily on the goat's neck and with one gruesome chop splashing blood everywhere.

Before that act of cold blooded slaughter, the painful, desperate whining of the goat begging for life, was unbearable.

That scene still lingers in my memory. I wondered to myself, how would it be if a human soul were to be chased and tied before his or her murder? Is this whine and dine? Should we make an animal whine before it becomes a desirable item for supper? Would I enjoy now a meat meal. Would I enjoy it if it is endorsed as an offering of human flesh after such a barbaric act?

This was a cue, a warning —that I have done enough damage to animal species and killed them indirectly, by feeding myself on them. These vulnerable beings have caused us no harm but have only beautified our surroundings and been a great resource. Witnessing a hen being hacked to death was the final act that convinced me to stop eating meat, poultry, fish. These beautiful creations of God are to be admired.

I am told that in some foreign lands, -may be in some places here too, buying fish is incomplete without buying raw fish by the seaside, which the fishermen caught in their fishing nets, while the fish flapped, kicked and breathed its last and the buyers watched gleefully. There was no one to mourn their death as they were unwanted, unadmired. In all likelihood, they would be baked, curried, barbequed on hot burning charcoal or browned ; if it were to be performed on humans it would be heinous crime.

For me the compelling reason for giving up non-vegetarian food was the thought that the animals were being sacrificed for the benefit of humans, when they too had a right to live and to have a natural death like us. They too feel pain and pleasure and love companionship. Cows, goats and in fact many harmless animals that we eat are vegetarians themselves ; they are attached to the persons who care for them and they reciprocate the care and affection showered on them.

Vegetarianism has givin me better health and good energy, giving me food containing proteins, carbohydrates, vitamins, iron, fat, all required to attain good health.

In many countries like ours, the Prevention of Cruelty to Animals Act prohibits infliction of cruelty on dogs and cats. But pigs and poultry and even goats grown on farms have no such protection, they can be straight away taken to slaughter houses. Eggs from mother hen are prevented from growing into a chick from the womb of the hen. Dogs and cats are cherished as companions; animals on farms are no less intelligent or capable of feeling pain or suffering.

Look at some famous vegetarians- Mahatma Gandhi, Bernard Shaw, Thomas Edison, Albert Einstein, Bill Clinton, Amitabh Bachan, Steve Jobs to name a few.

The temptation of eating an occasional non-vegetarian meal was strong in me for some time, but slowly and steadily I dared myself to overcome it. The decision rewarded me-I felt immense contentment the day I felt free from the urge for toxic meat meals. In due time this helped me to cook simple vegetarian meals at home, so that when I did see a grazing cattle, a herd of goats or a flock of wandering innocent animals I didn't feel guilty. I learnt to respect their space, their privacy, their natural habitats and familiar surroundings.

I felt a big burden of regret and worthlessness lifted off my shoulders, feeling closer to the animals once I turned a vegetarian, appreciating them as a boon than as a curse. They will feel closer to us if they are not slashed, tied, beaten or whipped. The point is not whether they can reason or talk. The point is that they do suffer. There is little difference between people convicted for animal cruelty and people indulging in violence against humans ; studies have shown that decreasing animal abuse will decrease domestic violence as the baseline is to inflict pain and suffering to another being, be it out of one's own greed, sadism or selfish satisfaction of other needs.

A vegetarian lifestyle awakens a spirit of compassion and empathy in me wishing that a kinder, gentler society may exercise a moral choice to protect animals rather than exploit them. Beneath the flesh and meat they too have an inner being, pleading for freedom, walking down the meadows where they unite with nature, when baby calf can nestle upto his mother and find pure joy in magical moments that are not for humans alone.

CHAPTER 15

JACKY I WISH I COULD CALL MY OWN

The basic requirement of everyone is something or someone to care for. To some, a pet is that 'someone' who brings in a balance, a new dimension, even a reason for living. I have observed people staying alone where pets have banished thoughts of loneliness by providing constant companionship.

I have been petrified of dogs. The bark alone gives me the jitters and irritates my senses. I am irked by the way their hair gets scattered all round the house. But I have always admired a well groomed, well trained dog, though more in the neighbour's home than in mine. Loving a pet dog from a distance was the closest I could get through to feel some affection for this species. On the one hand I would hear stories of how people were administered painful, detestable injections after dog bites-aggravating my fears and ruining any chances of a growing friendship with dogs as a whole-and on the other, I would hear of a story of an ailing woman, bedridden, who was saved at the nick of time, from the jaws of death, by her dog who fetched a doctor to revive her and give her a new lease of life. The story was that the lady was now up on her feet and walked her dog down in the park with renewed vigour, with a deep sense of gratitude to her pet, that was like a son she had longed for.

I was in a dilemma: was a dog just a ferocious animal incapable of feelings waiting to pounce on innocent lives? or was it a sincere and loyal companion to humans?. Our next door friend was bringing up a a fierce looking dog. It had two blazing eyes reminding me of police dogs, depicted as ruthless, as tracking criminals, knawing at them, biting with their sharp canines. Jacky was his name. He was pampered by his owners who treated him like a child. My neighbor spoke in Malayalam with him and tastefully fed him with drumstick sambar; Jacky would lap it all up, chew at the drumstick as though it was a tantalizing bone he had discovered. On days when a puja or a ceremony was conducted, Jacky would wag its furry tail, waiting to be smeared with sandalwood paste or with the bhasm or the holy grey ashes on the forehead. He was famous for his clowning, throwing up a dotty ball up in the air catching it and popping it up again with his posterior end, wriggling and dancing holding the ball in both the hands, trotting on his two feet like a ballet dancer to give it to his masters to say 'This is the prize i've won specially for you'. He would have easily won a dog show with the coveted crown on his head, delighting his proud owners.

Jacky belonged to my friend, Smita. When she was unwell, Jacky would lie by her side all day, for long abstaining from food or water holding on to the end of her bed linen and he would do this till she recovered. The family would get as concerned of Jacky as they were of Smita. He had an authoritative bark that invited a huge fan following, attracting other dogs to park themselves at our building gate as though Jacky was presiding over a general body meeting. My son was extremely fond of him and nicknamed him Boboo. He would stroke his thick mane, laugh at his antics and whisper sweet nothings into his ears in a language of their own. My little son would protest against the collar chain and the leach that was tied round his neck that chased him around. Though not particularly a lover of dogs, I still likened this to a man being lifted with a noose tied round his neck, to be strangled to death. More so, because Jacky would strain his neck out obediently, let the collar be strapped on to his neck and follow in whichever direction he was taken.

Jacky didn't try to grab my attention, provoke or scare me, knowing well that I feared him. He had sensed that not once had I expressed any love for him when he almost asked to be smothered, to be stroked or held fondly by me. In a sense, Jacky was more human and touchable than I could ever be, so I judged.

I think these thoughts started working on me. Gradually I began to reach out to him, I felt like shaking hands and petting his cute snubbed nose. Jacky was truly sensitive. Once I dared to pat him, he slowly walked past me silently, knowing that I was still hesitant to approach him and that hurt him. Just then, our neighbour's son was heard screaming from the garden sounding panic stricken and mortally fearful of a huge king cobra advancing slowly towards him as he was riding his bicycle. Jacky's bark resembled a loud roar and he mounted on the bench the little boy and shielded him till the snake found its way into its pit. Jacky was the hero of the evening. His timely help and judgement, was a life saving effort. As a reward Jacky was given rich dog biscuits and extra lip tickling bones!

One moonlit night, Jacky was heard howling unusually mournfully as though he was in deep anguish. It was a warning, we thought: a signal that some thing grave was about to happen. All the more because the lady of the house was battling with a terminal illness and the end could have come any day. Not long after, the lady breathed her last. She was very attached to Jacky and so was he to her. He found it difficult to cope with the tragedy and moaned for days on end. He finally whined for the last time in exasperation, gasping for breath, succumbing to an untimely death. He was loyal to his master in her waking hours and so in her death.

To my regret, I had awakened too late to connect with an animal that yearned to be petted, that had a heart. And, may be a soul. That soul still haunts me- makes me realise that dogs are sincere and faithful ; a rarity in today's world. No wonder then that they are known as man's best friend! I was deeply grieved and disturbed by the thought that not even once did I try getting close to Jacky who displayed as much humaneness and selfless love, as humans did. A pet I wished I could have called my own.

Chapter 16

What Makes Us One

*"We have enough religion to make us hate,
but not enough to make us love one another"*

Jonathan Swift

What makes us one!

During visits to the Church, the temple, the mosque and the Gurudwara I've observed a strange sense of peace, rejuvenation that multitudes of worshippers get from them and their ceremonies, preachings and pujas. It is the power of love and the love of Almighty that perhaps induces devotees to throng to various places of worship.

I believe in attempting direct communication with the Almighty rather than the indirect route of rituals, rites and rites performers. When one religion separates one community from another and religions form several folds, intolerance of another's religion often spreads hatred and religious hatred makes the unseen Almighty unseeable and ignored. For all our human activity no one needs to ask who belongs to which sect or religion. We humans have the same blood running through us and echo similar sentiments, the same lamp shines in all of us, the lamp that lights up our hearts and minds, the lamp that can lead to a holy communion of souls. From every move we make and every breath we take.

The mystical lamp is lit everywhere, the holy water is sprinkled as an offering, the ashes are smeared on the forehead. The similarities are many although the ideals, procedures are different. The ultimate aim of everyone is to wear an ornament of peace and harmony. When we cover our head with a scarf, a saree or a turban as a mark of respect to the Almighty, why can't we think that our brothers and sisters, our close ones are apparitions of the Almighty uniting us into one huge family of this wondrous world? We can enjoy the same space and share the same freedom to voice opinions without hurting one another. Instead of teaching each other the do's and don'ts, we need compassionate guides to protect and shelter us from the cold vibes and the scorching arguments, from fanaticism and dogma.

In the name of religion, gross malpractices are conducted, poor creatures are butchered as sacrifice to heavenly power and innocent babies beheaded as offerings; atrocities like shaving the head of widowed women rob them of their good looks, their right to live and progress. The culprits are released, go scot free and these inhuman acts are attributed to the demands and rules of religion. Are these human sacrifices, massacres and tortures pleasurable, exciting or worthwhile? That leaves a baggage of guilt, dishonour and disbelief in us.

Positive thoughts and the will to spread and goodness are present in all of us. People from different religious groups assemble to celebrate festivals, weddings, cricket matches and other events of common interest when all differences are forgotten and persons embrace, and express genuine love for each other. Such bonding sets the tear glands flowing and one thinks of the unity that underlies all diversity. This feeling of oneness, can bring people closer to universal love.

To me the only saint who lives in our hearts and minds is the Almighty. He has sent his messengers, living saints who with their wisdom and knowledge can make us surrender ourselves to the will of Divinity. These messengers are the blessed ones. What brings us together is the thread of common link with the Almighty ; the power of love and the will to follow love as the only religion above everything else. True devotees can be identified as followers of Allah, Bhagwan, Jesus, Guru Nanak and so forth, who pledge their devotion to the one and only Lord and Master, the light of love who resides in us, to awaken the Holy Spirit of supremacy within.

The world of love and compassion towers over the rules of religion.

Love is the magical word, uniting people of all religions. True affections are explained better in expressions than in suppressions. The Religion of love is our saviour, our messiah; we discard pieces of untold miseries, that rock the foundations of meaningful existence, and learn to love not one religion, but all religions. Shall we hope for a day, in the not very distant future, when a little child would seek to know what his religion is and and would simply know that he is part of this magnificent creation of humankind and lives a life scripted and directed by the the Creator himself?.

Chapter 17

Searching for the Divinity Within- Notes To Myself

"The most sacred place isn't the church, the mosque or the temple, it's the temple of the body. That's where spirit lives."

Susan L Taylor.

Spirituality is a soul searching experience to me, a journey into the inner self, opening the gates to freedom, to seek the truth about oneself, while connecting the spirit within with the master spirit without. This focuses on the black, grey and white shades of human tendencies, of discovering newer dimensions of human life, looking deeper into the recesses of the heart, the goodness of the inner self uniting spiritual awakening with the magnificent gifts of the materialistic world. Spirituality is not a religion to me, but a genuine approach to recognising the essential goodness in all persons including the self. I am satisfied and more peaceful when I find room for further growth in me than when I dwell in the improved state that has come about.

In miserable moments, I have easily been inflicted by negative thoughts and these have as easily been translated into negative actions. The mind then gets ruled by the terror of pessimism, making every notion appear unreasonable ; looking as if there is no return to the earlier state of contentment. In happier moments, on the other hand, I am easily convinced that I can reach great levels of satisfaction, well above what I can reach normally with what little I possess.

Just when I believe that I have nothing more to achieve, a new challenge crops up needing my attention, to yet again ready myself for a new travel in life, to learn with massive renewed effort. Feeling the burden of erratic thoughts, I would then imagine that I have to do many things in a short time and that would add pressure to the existing tension, making living difficult, throwing a huge weight on my slender shoulders.

Every time I fall off from a height I believe there is still hope for me for the better, while stuttering on the steps to the same height, putting in fresh efforts to light the candle to a new promise and a new purpose.

It is said that what is good for one may not be good for another but I find that universal love has an overwhelming appeal to everyone irrespective of caste, creed, country or even religion. I need the strength and the support that can be obtained from within, to set and steadfastly follow the direction I so much desire in life, but that support slips away when I fail to connect with the paramount saviour. Perhaps that happens when I fail to strike a balance between spiritual gratification and materialistic gains. (Is there such a balance? if there is how does one discover it?)

At times, the Almighty's answers to my prayers are delayed; they disappoint me when I expect to be rewarded immediately; my wish is granted when I patiently wait; I try to receive it with gratitude and value it without taking anything for granted. I believe in destiny but also believe that I need to oil the wheels of progress to achieve my goals, to shoulder responsibility that comes with maturity and to change for the better according to my knowledge of the commands of destiny. Sometimes it is difficult for me to realise situations and their depths, perhaps due to circumstantial pressures or constraints. But I find I can have the resolve to live without distractions by concentrating on my present than confining myself to an irrelevant past or planning too much about the future - that can cause avoidable anxiety and unrest.

Do I give my Self as my first priority or am I keen on pleasing multitudes of people before getting self satisfaction. To my knowledge I come first : unless I love and accept myself as I am I can't be of help to anyone else. So it is necessary for me to understand myself first, often pardon and forgive and be good to myself, be sensitive to my own feelings and others. I may understand my life's motive to better myself but I may have flaws ; I need to remind myself that I am not perfect, not an idol or a saint, but am human, with human frailties, with a deep wish not to make the same errors again and again. I feel the Lord, my master, who is the picture of perfection will guide me in my life's mission.

If I could reach out to even a few people and make them happy I would be blessed and consider myself lucky. When I recline back and dwell in unwanted past experiences, the feeling of present growth in me gets stunted and conflicting, the desire to go on is replaced by mental stagnation and immobility, blocking work which ought to be put in for further growth. Doctors too drive home the message that most illnesses are cured with love and prayers, the true medicines to heal the diseases of the mind and body. Pain and pleasure as I see are the two sides of the same coin: intervening pleasure makes long stretches of pain bearable but pain itself is the outcome of pleasure and pleasure the outcome of pain.

At times when my mind is clouded with unnecessary thoughts, with constant prayers, I feel the presence of the Divine Grace within me and I try to concentrate on performing my duties to better my thought processes according to the commands of the merciful Lord. I need to speak well, think sensibly to ward off the unpleasantness that corrodes the mind. This will be a life long mission.

I am trying to be tolerant with difficult situations "and relationships and I expect less from people than I used to. I am trying to learn to accept them as they are. However, following this always is not easy when my ego rebels -but gets a sound beating -when I don't get my way or when my wish is ignored or disregarded. When I am hungry I eagerly wait for my turn to be served and when my hunger is satisfied, the craving for the want disappears. But when I thirst for life and its miracles, I thirst for the magic that life unfolds even after quenching my thirst, the craving is more and knows no end. I sometimes query as to why happiness is snatched away from me, only to fathom that all good ends with the coming of trying periods, which is yet again followed by happy times ; the changes are like the dashing waves of the sea climbing over one another.

I often fear myself more than I fear the Almighty who needs to be loved than feared ; I fear that I may fall short of my own expectations ; I fear the Unknown and the Uncertain ; this keeps me agile and active most of the time. Despite upheavals it's worth living as life often draws parallels with a seemingly true -to -life movie highlighting the good vs the evil, enjoying the song and dance sequences to project merriment and joy, becoming euphoric at the birth of a being, and dramatising a tragic death in the end. A little spice, a little sweetness can cause a spectacular and colourful twist to an ordinary dull existence.

CHAPTER 18

PANGS OF SEPARATION

"Love is the only reality and it isnot merely sentiment. It is the ultimate truth that lies at the heart of creation."

Kalyani R Menon

It was like yesterday. I went through once again a gamut of emotions, experiencing pangs of separation in full measure. Separation from our dear ones for long periods by distance can be excruciatingly painful. At the same time living apart taught me some important lessons that, I am sure, many others have already learnt. It could be separation between husband and wife when they are in different places; when one is left as the sole parent playing the role of father and mother; or at other times, separation of parents from children when the child grows up in the confines of a boarding school or a hostel.

For many years, I lived in India while my husband worked in Muscat, basically for better job satisfaction and monetary benefits. We could unite only once a year. This brought newness, a freshness to our home, to us, a thirsting for love that waited longingly, love that was unspoken yet understood. We knew that we had to stay apart, that we lived in two different worlds, yet the dividing line only increased the understanding between two individuals, even two families, and us. The fact that this union was to be short increased our sense of togetherness. We were physically apart but the unity in mind increased our fondness for each other and it matured to pack off petty squabbles and to know each other's mind, needs and emotions, even in the absence of much verbal communication.

I often thought of several thousand women staying away from their spouses, waiting for that magnificent rainbow to reappear and bring occasionally color and magic into their lives. I thought of the courage and strength of mind they had in managing their homes and their children and to seek an inner sense of well being when their husbands were away for long spells. Sometimes distance can cause deep depression, and the need to consult a counselor or a psychiatrist to gain emotional stability. The question that often arose in my mind was: was marriage just the seven rounds taken of the holy pyre to certify people as man or wife? Does it merely address a need to stay together until the candle blows out and you fade into oblivion.? Living apart from compulsion rather than choice makes one feel worthless at times.

Separation often leads to acute anxiety when the distress it causes is not within manageable limits. As a woman is separated from one on whom she is woefully dependent this anxiety often has negative effects on social and emotional functioning, on family life and physical health. I too have had that experience. Yet I used to tell my husband: "You are too far to embrace but too near to my pining heart to love." Missing him was a painful experience, but I was reassured that he would come home someday, so the negativity dissolved to make our marriage sweeter and days memorable. Our hearts remained inseparable when the oceans and borders weren't obstacles but a source of rejuvenation of the mind, when living beyond separation was a challenge to overpower the effects of trauma; to remember only sweeter moments of togetherness rather than to watch the calendar waiting desperately for the recognizable knock on the door. To proclaim love is easy, but can we stand up to its intensity and pain during difficult times? A true test of our strength? True love triumphs, when we are back together pardoning our shortcomings and displaying our strengths, when each day, every moment, seems precious to us to share positive energies with each other, to be safe, happy and responsible to each other, to be wanted by each other.

With my husband by my side I no more fear the pangs of separation as I am learning to respect and treasure him. It was through separation that we learnt to understand problems, and uncertainties and valued and appreciated the quality time we had spent during short, very sweet intervals in our life. During the first fifteen years of our married life.

In human relationships I learnt distances are not measured in miles but in affection. We may live together yet be miles apart. So we've decided to explore the world hand in hand putting in that extra effort to be united, putting the pangs of separation behind us, relishing every minute of that blessedness we get by the divine grace of the Almighty.

You are so far, yet so close, barred by distances bonded by love. Its not what we do but the little things we do together, that brings us joy Those who travel afar know whether the journey is worth a wait. Cherish and appreciate everything and everyone, as what is today is gone tomorrow. Fascinations subside not the will to survive.

CHAPTER 19

WHEN THE JOURNEY
SEEMS ENDLESS

This is a plea, an outcry from surviving women, and children to help prevent monstrous attacks and advances from retarded men that demoralise and destroy the basic sanctity of womanhood. Physical assaults leave permanent scars, wounding the mind and body and to add further insult, families, society and prospective grooms shun the very path these women walk. Indeed their state becomes the collective guilt of society.

We need two hands to clap, the one who provokes and the one who is provoked. Some provocative dresses, designed to often entice men, invite trouble; dressing pleasantly helps protect one's chastity by keeping the beastly attacks at bay. On the other hand, when people are starved, and overpowered by uncontrollable desire, they seek the forbidden, despite societal pressures and rules. This is when a relatively decently dressed woman or an innocent child becomes a victim of lust and unjust craving. The man furious at not getting what he wants, grabs forcibly what is not his, with aggression, without reasoning or thought.

When there are increasing numbers of men waiting for an opportunity to be driven into such a heinous crime, can a woman walk through lonely streets without fear that some mentally deranged person may pounce upon her and cause permanent injury to her body and mind. There is no room for reasoning when the man over powers and chips the feathers of the woman who in despair and disbelief remains silent and motionless reeling under the shock ; only to relive the torrid past many times, for many years, to lead a lifetime of anguish and utter misery.

It is sad and shocking that some women and children, for no fault of theirs, are subjected to physical abuse, that their desperate moans are muffled by meaningless social noise. Can the victims face the world after being brutally assaulted? They run from pillar to pillar crying for help, for justice only to find all doors slammed against them. We often hear of the unbearable shame and its ending in suicide.

This deadly game may make the man feel victorious, defeating a helpless lady who surrenders totally under his control and power -as if a timid creature is chased by a fierce animal and would wait for the final call of death than be alive with a huge and permanent stigma.

Added to this, the media sometimes provides excessive coverage of such unfortunate events-but the more the exposure, the curiosity to unearth facts which may be bizarre or distorted, the deeper the misery of the victims. In some houses they are disowned, unwanted by their own flesh and blood. Where could these homeless, helpless children of the Almighty go? Could they weave a safe nest and fly away? Who will remove the curse from their lives when they have already paid a heavy price, and need understanding, empathy and love than ever before from the loved ones. They require social and family acceptance and support from the community to learn to live their lives once again. Instead life becomes revengeful, and the victim waits for a chance to punish the gamblers of destiny who have wrecked their lives. When the aggrieved is blessed with the right to live, the will to live increases, reducing the hatred towards oneself, reducing self blame -that she has in some way been responsible for the gruesome incident.

In some cases the individual, and the party to the crime are convicted and put behind the bars. Will this solve the problem? It is a deplorable mental sickness which has to be treated, deeply rooted in the mind due to a variety of causes: maybe dissatisfaction, lack of confidence, lack of self- control, some hidden complex or plain derangement. Similarly the victims need to be treated for being listless, for having guilt pangs, just as the men need to be.

I wish to fly into the blue sky. Swung to land forcibly into the green meadows desolate and deserted, releasing an escaping gasp of inconsolable tears. Is it real or is it a nightmare? None would answer, neither the fragrant flowers nor the river flowing by. The sun, the trees and the birds witness the plight, merciless and forbidden. Draped in scattered pieces of linen, given a life to be torn apart, will she live to see the moonshine? She is not sorry for yesterday, <u>tomorrow</u> is a distant dream, what is meaningful is her today. All she wishes is peace and tranquility, to savour its sweetness as a priceless gift from heaven.

Printed in the United States
By Bookmasters